Radio, Radio

BEN DOYLE •——

RADIO, RADIO

• POEMS

LOUISIANA STATE UNIVERSITY PRESS   BATON ROUGE

2001

Designer: Laura Roubique Gleason
Typeface: Minion text with Orator display
Printer and binder: Thomson-Shore, Inc.

Library of Congress Cataloging-in-Publication Data

Doyle, Ben.
    Radio, radio : poems / Ben Doyle.
        p.   cm.
    ISBN 0-8071-2678-0 (cloth : alk. paper) — ISBN 0-8071-2679-9 (paper : alk.
paper)
    I. Title.

PS3554.O97428 R34 2001
811'.6—dc21
                                                    00-048554

The author gratefully acknowledges the editors of the following publications, in
which some of the poems herein first appeared, sometimes in slightly different
form: *American Poet, Boston Review, Colorado Review, Fence, Iowa Journal of Cul-
tural Studies, New Republic, Open City, Tin House,* and *Web Conjunctions.*

Thanks to the many Doyles, Lewis Turco, James Harms, Lyn Hejinian, Mark
Levine, Jim Galvin, Jorie Graham, and the Braille Drivers. Thank you Susan Howe.

The paper in this book meets the guidelines for permanence and durability of the
Committee on Production Guidelines for Book Longevity of the Council on Li-
brary Resources. ∞

Cover image: The telemetric egg was designed by George Stetten and used at the
Bronx Zoo to study the natural incubation of the White Naped Crane. The device
measures temperature, humidity, and egg orientation while being cared for in the
nest by unsuspecting birds. For more information, visit www.stetten.com.

WINNER OF THE WALT WHITMAN AWARD FOR 2000

Sponsored by The Academy of American Poets, the Walt Whitman Award is given annually to the winner of an open competition among American poets who have not yet published a book of poems.

Judge for 2000: Susan Howe

to Brette

CONTENTS

RADIO, RADIO

Still Life

This must be what I meant to tell you:
nothing is nothing new, o my goddess, o my goodness,
the pandemonium fits on the head of a pin
whose body is within the body of a poisoned
poison red moth.

Make that a billion pandemoniums, each the size
of a panic, an attack, the echoing decay; an idea.
Clouds of mothdust form around the gilded arch
as they hurl themselves against it . . . desperate sex.
They are breaking or broken. One good wing
beats for both
                    —tailspin.

Over five billion served & still I have hunger & heartburn,
still my table is trashed, unset, still my booth too big.

Still churchwindows are made with no defrosters,
still cameras come without safetyswitches

& a great pandemonium is still silently processing [word, food]
the still, static city. Outside the outskirts the leaky distillery
& the feral mammals, sipping, snarling & stumbling
in a clearing where wild drunken roses sway like moths on ammonia.

In all of the photos my eyes are this color.

Cerise-centered. Sanguine outline.

Satellite Convulsions

When I bend back to gaze at the satellite convulsions, I
am an aqueduct for twilit rain. Quite literally I stand

in the littoral zone: a lens—no, an aqueous humor, my
feet on the land below the high-water mark, my hand

a glazed waver: *hello light-purple lights, hello red spots,*
you've beaten the stars out tonight but you're struggling with the

atmosphere, ain't ye? Over centuries the river became not
a river: Lethe's ends crept together—self-scavenging sea

snake—& the middle filled with water—morphology dubbed it
a lake & now the moon swims in it & the moon orbits it &

the moon tidally tugs on it. The moon is a satellite in a fit
of paroxysm. One minute past, I emptied an aluminum can

of dull opiate to the drains to wash down my antipsychotics
& then Lethe-wards slunk I. There must be this wire shaking

loose in my mind, an unattended firehose, a spasmodic
filament attempting to cool the baby planet but lacerating

precious gray matter. Thought leaves no vacancy for memory—
I forget & forget the rules, the thirst an auger, rain only whetting

it, I bend & lap some lake up, tongue it, suck the silty mammary
right where a light from the firmament meets it. I keep forgetting

the rules, a Ptolemaniac with stars & suns circling me; I keep
missing my cues, can't arrange the particles moments are made of—

and it's all good!—because when I bend seriously back & peep
at the satellite convulsions I am a sluiceway for night rain. If I love

at least I love aptly, terminally, like a man who loves his dinner until
he's done with it, then settles to the couch to easy pixilated dreams

(bounced off, yes, satellites, & beamed into a pale dish). And still,
even unfettered by history or hope, the world does not seem

shocking—simply something to fly a canvas balloon around, to
dig a hole in. To climb into. To allow to fill with water, perhaps

it is raining, perhaps you dig below the watertable; it gushes through
the dirt; your bath is drawn & in it are drawn (sputniks & stars) maps

& charts with which to constellate your body. Connect the dots.
A little ladle with four handles—a tiny light strobes in the cup, in hot

convulsions of distance, bleats of temporal ignorance, synapse of morse
but no code, blood but no pulse, the stream but no mouth or source.

Recess in the Forest

There was a small disaster,
west of here, minutes ago,
I know there was: a pink
& gold ribbon blew from
a schoolgirl's hair & deep
inside a thornbush. A timid
half-wild Appaloosa kept its
distance on the other side
of the planet, slowly licking
rainwater from inside a tire.
The tractor splayed on its back
at the bottom of a mooncrater.

Alas! if only I was there now,
I could name that very horse,
give it a shard of saltrock.
I could easily turn that tractor upright—
so small the gravity is there.

But I am here: thorn through
my tongue, thorn through my temple,
thorn in my thigh dreaming.

Tug

The tug on my arm but soon spread
Perhaps now they could prove me there.

I've been watching the sky closely & for some time,
My hands in it, making crude, beautiful doves.

Sometimes a sprinkler spits
An arc of silver water over me,

Hissing, bisecting. Half of a thing
As much of a thing as ever can be.

If they have to water it, it's not a real field.
It's a yard, connected to a white building.

Once, I was inside a building.
Tooth, your shadow the color of the hour.

•

There was a smell of some spice,
I don't know what it was called.
I wanted to take a bath, change my gravity;
Feel my skin loose & leave a ring.
The man said they only had shower stalls.
Those were the days everyone lived
In fear of a fierce spouse,
Paddling through the steam,
Something in her hand:
Hair-dryer, toaster, leaf-blower,
Plugged-in & zinging.

And you there, stewing in your own
Sauce, whistling an oldie.

•

Deaf by dawn & if dawn comes
Day may break—bellowing
Below thing, be low, sing,
Slinging blows, blowing slang
Songs, bowing. Bring out the big
Amp, vinyl torn, plywood exposed,
I think the tubes are ready, sir,
The dew I flicked on them leapt & left

•

Steelsleet, the weather from the recycle tower
Less yellow as it lowers, a film of it tinting
The buildings, tinning the yards with first light.

I've seen the hours of train from above on the bridge,
Each car brimmed with rusty blades, broken bayonets,
Naked bent frames of things . . . I can't tell. . . .

Can you smell the crimson? And the cars behind me,
Metal mixed at the proper ratio, careen dying to be there,
Gasoline hemorrhaging, pistons punching themselves out.

The barge gravid with metal took its miles to pass as I stood
On the bank not saluting, thinking *now, now what am I going to do.*

The first blast of the opening ore-oven decays all decay.
The scraps shine. The smelting starts seamless, top down, bottom up.
Hollowing. Hello, thing. Hell, lathing. Howlingly singing holes.

•

So what are you going to be?
   —A ghost.
I stole a white sheet from a line.
Leaves were stuck to it, I'll
Punch some holes in it, I'll
Jump from the balconies
Of bleached buildings

The War Is Over

Not an acquiescence of surrender,
the bra hung from the flagpole.

The bra is black & there is no wind for once.
For once there is no wind & a spark that is a bird
brings a straw to an empty C-cup. A spark

that is a spark. That is the sun on the steel pole.
That is the oldest thing & then is gone, like the war,

whose trench is gone, because it is full of
red iron-clot soil, because there are lawnchairs
reclined on top of it (empty, but warm, still warm,

sweat-wet & stretched-out) & a white plastic table
with a pitcher of dark iced tea upon it.

The ice is half melted. Clear water waits near the brim.
The wasp waving in it annoys a piece of dust so minute
it might not be there. In its head is only enough space

for a split second of a song it heard the third of July, a trombone belch
muted with a pink plunger-head. The war was over again,
the parade began hitchless, history was history, a refugee

pinned a Purple Heart on a brave bomb & a drop of brown
blood rolled down its chest like a tumbling tumbleweed

as the saints came marching in in white fur hats, in white plastic
shoes, in tuxedoes matching the color-scheme of decrepit glory,
glockenspieled, anacondad in sousaphones, a trombone

with a wasp on its brass bell resting its wings.
It is pausing on my reflection, midtone, in the center of my stain.

Then there is the snapshot of the sky departing generously,
perhaps forever. Appropriately dark, we finally see the "grand finale"
& realize it is only the preceding parts pushed closely together

& we think we are all a bit relieved,
although we are afraid to admit even this.

Code

There were these times—who now can truly say?— when
even to be lightly walked upon would begin the reaction—
& by the smallest of pests, mere, a mere dot, a fool's jewel.

Or even times we misinterpreted the signal from the turret:
the wedding smoke a cloak of crank, a maze, a call to arms.

And, bracers crooning our depth perception into a cool wash,
we would begin our descent into the glossy valley, kicking
lichens backward to scramble our path. Our faces matted

with mosses, our torches hissing at both ends, we crept on our bellies
into the village's thoroughfare this way, splintering the dress rehearsal.

And so it was, until one of them guffawed. And so it was,
until one stood & directed us to the friends-of-the-bride section,
which sat empty on that side, save the hired immigrant family.

And we, we who were too humiliated to continue: when we could have
taken them then—in their revelry & surprise—we sat, we sat down.
          And we wailed. For curious love & a union of convenience.

How we wish now they would give us back our things!
For what is this liberty, truly, without the effigies of our wealth,
to polish, to burn, & to burn for our selves?

Returning, & humbled, we shot scions from their tallest, straightest,
most vigorous timber. We tried to graft them to the young
sprigs rooted in our sopping seed-orchard, we tried.

Not to say that the blight was directly caused by this,
but the timing, could it be only coincidence?

Praise be, praise be to the occluded genetic ladders, whose
                                        rungs are blind to us,
bedimmed by clouds, intestinal clouds, now gone blue & black.
We see your spots. And we blow into our vacant palms,
in preparation for a dustless climb.

As the man says, we must either diminish our wants or augment
our means. But that man, he has everything: he's dead.

From *The Selected & New Stories of S.*
The Mailman [from *Worldworks*]

A one with a thousand zeroes after it
is such an infinitely tiny number I can't
even believe we're discussing it, he said,
moving his mouth. Terrible, terrible mouth.

I thought he was gonna pull me on top
of him & try to kiss me. That's not my bag.
I was made to please the ladies.
I had all these little skeletons in my pockets.

So I began to count zeroes silently,
deep inside my cloroxed skull.
And wait for him to relax. He's right,
it's hard to count zeroes, even if

you make up a little story a mnemonic device
about the zeroes like this zero
went to the park & took off all
her clothes except her golden bra.

Underneath the bra her breasts
were like two perfect zeroes,
breasts we had hidden in the park
like ground spiders to gaze upon.

Just then the skeletons began to strum
their ribs together, a riotous music they made,

the egg the mailman was sitting on
hatched into a spray of green wires
& he ran back into his idling white hearse,
a zero wrapped inside a larger one.

The Canary Islands

I say I see satellitic ribbons working at the corners of it.
You say you see leguminous vetchlings twining up the side
Of my building & they twitch just a little on its big belly.
We whisper our vespers barely discernible from the sound
Of the jackhammers perforating the street & our vespers
Mean whatever they might, providing said vespers are gibbered.
So, sad, unostentatious vespers for us & the distending
Shadows of some formidable new clouds. You say are we not
& I say yes we are & often the man whose prayers fill the alleys,
Papa, his head is out the window, he's screaming something.
He's spitting.

I say I can't tell what Papa is screaming. Is that another language?
Yes. Spanish, you say. We're from the Canary Islands.

Remember the ship, the white sail that turned deep red overnight;
My lone true love, garroted?

And now you're crying & cursing at me in Spanish, *Español*—
Language I dreamed in in Barcelona with seeds in my curls,
Language I whispered in Tenochtitlán as white sparks
                              cracked from the bridge—
Such specific verbs that I know I am being scolded, my specialty,
                              my beloved.

There sure are a lot of twigs on the street, considering
There isn't a single tree in this city. Not a tree not a tree in the city.
What color is that beneath the vetch? I would have to say orange.
But a different kind of orange, the darkest imaginable.
Almost a sienna. The color of so many bricks, vines glued
Suggestively. Vines with swollen pods weighing them down
Like bags of sand outside the wicker basket of a hot-air balloon.

Now I remember the Canary Islands—
The tide falling in from every direction,
I remember hiding among the adolescent corn, a child myself.
Caked with black mud, the salt sucked from my sleeve,
A cloud of black feathers; a white mare that could race in your hand.

Papa is strapping something heavy to his head, exasperated.
He's whittling a sharp point on the end of an ashen stick.
The compass twists from the hollow hilt of his gap-toothed knife.
Papa, who once spent a night in a down bag.

Papa gots to get paid.

I don't know what to tell you, you've already sold your hair.
Here, try these & tell me if they're actually beans.

And on the first day,

the telephone cord snapped
from overuse. It was everywhere.
The refrigerator stopped its petulant
knocking; in the abandoned mailbag
I found the following letter:

chickenscratch in chickenscratch
in chickenscratch.

And on the second day,

all dogs I had considered adopting
                at the pound had been
"put to sleep."
A drift of white fur was still
                in the corner of a cage;
I hid it in my mouth.

And on the third day,

we mated furiously on a cardboard mat
while the calico goldfish Marco looked on
levitating in his jumbo bell jar.
I knew soon we would say the awful thing
that would tether us like horses to saloons,
so I went inside & bought a bottle of sour mash.

Later:
I stepped through the rip in your screendoor
& snuck Marco under your pillow as you slept
the huge sleep of someone

who had made a decision to, in the morning,
decide.

And on the fourth day,

it was overcast &
I awoke only in time for about an hour of that.
My clock-radio had become deprogrammed in an
electrical storm.
I wasn't sure if noon was a.m. or p.m.,
& then those data seemed very important.
Open to suggestions, I wandered to town
with a virgin credit card
singing "alleluia, alleluia" in my breast pocket.

p.s.: The sun was behind the green tarp.

And on the fifth day,

I mowed the lawn with a hangover.
I poisoned a three-point line
with used motor oil into the shorn grass
surrounding the concrete square
& worked on my jumper
until the clouds drew whistles.

And on the sixth day,

a vault arched through the sky
& created a sunset somewhere new.
I scurried under the coffee table
like a crab who has seen the future

& on the seventh day,

it is the seventh day.

The New Season

1

First the deconditioning of the dogs:
stuff them with steak for weeks then offer them
a fruit cocktail, coat their hides with honey
& run them through the seedling dandelion
fields, rob your own house while you sleep upstairs;
show them the footage of the pavlovian
experiments—the fork in the brain & its
corresponding drooly lake. All this &
still the dogs shall love you. So remove your
dress & dance with one in the den, its paws
on your shoulders, hands on its sprouting back—
look into those bewildered broke eyes, wild
how they are wilding, devolution made
so easy even I would consider—
in fact, beg you—to escort me, muzzled,
back through the fading yard, uncut whipgrass
cartographers scriving latitude lines
on our bare ankles, & when at last we
reach the post, please bind me to it & then
please give me a good solid one right here,
right where my crown should be, please, divide me
like the day, the age—

2

                make an example
out of me—show what becomes of someone
rabid with concerns concerning the fire-
works you keep inside your silk purse, the big
party you seem to be preparing for,
the fuses in your ears & the burning
house you are always at the threshold of,

love, peeling off your puppet & waving
to the train with two engines, each leaving
the station instantly in opposite
directions.

3

And the space in the air like
a stolen pie just before the sound splits
its dew point & the new season begins!

Dark Lantern

Terrifically twisted glitch that brought me here.
Long-distance luck or lack thereof.
Oh we had hints but they were pure
Hint: the dirty dish of milk, the silver scarab

Beetles drying totemic on every screendoor.
Darkness dehiscing, discharged stars in dejecta,
I lit my dark lantern but kept each louver
Choked. It made the black seem blacker, sharp trifecta

Of seams, beams so thin the lines on things
Made them more masked, unmanageable, more
Unimaginable than when we had only the tissue strings
Of our memories to tug on. And I felt both sure

That if I revealed more night night would break
Us & ashamed that we might have broken night.
Undeviating blank visibility here. The wake
Of verb to noun—three thin strips of light . . .

Meanwhile, our situation has been upgraded to
A "Situation." Sitzkrieg of the remaining senses.
The sear & stench of the sucked fuel from the flue
And wick wheezing like lungs lashed between tenses.

Meanwhile, our situation has been upgraded to a "Situation"

This stupid skiff won't get me to the gulf on time,
cries somehow up through its cracks, a baby on its back.

The yellow trees shush us. The orange ones bleed sweet crude.
Despite the salt the meat has molted & smells so.

Dead rushes rush space in the cutbank we're wedged in
the cutbank & may have mites, for they scratch ceaseless.

Yesterday, a monobrowed man dragging four bloody geese
waved a white kerchief at a hill. A black angus ate a snoopy kite.

Yesterday after that, a congaline of thunderstorms—
rerouting the ground-gashes—one lulled, one loomed

& now we're floating—thin trickle rinsing the parabolic gouge
below that let me down. So I sit & in my hands, I turn the stick.

My long useless stick, tracing the outline of the lone liver-shaped,
liverspotted cloud, dying. The edge of the lone sky. A thousand
          pardons, Herr Doktor, for I am only this big.

I know, I am the lone blemish in the enormous diamond that prompts the
          appraiser
To weep up his monocle. The hidden ribbon of yellow fat devastating the red jelly
          steak. The butcher throws his smock on the floor.

I am the man standing on an unfolding chair at the Little Miss pageant,
in the back of the elementary gymnasium, head in a net, pleading.

In the west the West is putting its towheaded child, the East, away.
Somebody do something. My logbook made of wet logs, waterlogged,

has smeared inside. If I had something for the pain, it would be gone.
The sisal tore at my palms. If it frosts tonight, the meat will still stink,

idiot nocturnals will crawl here with their claws & autumn disease.
Gibbering inside their tiny brains. If I had some soup I'd sip some soup
        from this shoehorn, for I hate to tie my shoes.

Long ago I promised myself not to be taken by an animal.
I can break a broom over my leg. I can kick, bite, like an animal; I promise to be
        wilder this time.

A cracked rock holds no fire. Rubbed two sticks raw together.
There's nothing I have grinning to burn the boat down.

Yesterday after that I was thinking, if I say I have no regrets,
I have no regrets. Already I knew it would be impossible to miss my life,

so charmless, so staid. And such memories. And so few. Oh my sweet girl,
Maude, wobbly on ice-skates; tiny blond Jeremy, bent into a tin tub—

a miracle: you stand with the water on your face gleaming, a huge waxy apple
damming your smile—of my regrets, two are you never being born.

Biplanes circle overhead & laugh at the flares I've scattered. Light fizzes.
I'm on a slide. They spray their gray dust at me, to keep me covered & queasy
        throughout the uninsulated night.

A banner unfurls. It might be my name, & other things, things written
in a picture language, one with no letters. Welcome to the orient, I say,
        the sky going red, embarrassed.

Here, it is just one place. Under every rock are baby adders & they make good
        pencil-mustaches
when I look in the stream. A thousand pardons, I forgot what a man was.

I forgot I had a mouth until I saw it there, under my mustache. It looks better
        open &
there's a bag in the back of my throat. Where I keep my cargo.

Ten Minutes

Why thank you, we grind them daily,
& are you going to the equinox festival?

White checker in the brunette grass, kissed with dirt.

No sir, I have not heard of equinox.

Sighting-target stickers on real-estate signs, piles.

O, where, where are you from?

And part of a house made from coffee brick bags, smells like coffee.

It smells like coffee here. Good coffee.

A necklace of grenade pins, a scabby tan.

Why thank you, we grind them daily, & are you
going to the equinox festival?

The strips of garden sawed into the side of the mountain.
The dung there, the humming green flies. The green clumps of bean husk.

No sir, I have not heard of equinox.

And the detectives, sharpening their machetes, smoking.
The thick-fallen vine that ceases into the pit.

Day & night are equal.

Lover's drained head on an oil drum, a lovely, pale warning.

Wow.

Tsunami of kudzu. Strands rising in parts,
beginning, just now, to shake off the cyclones.
The reptile legs of a wild turkey, nailed over the threshold.

Why thank you. It's why the caravans. The festive outfits.
Are you going? You'll be right on time. Are you going?

Glycerin bubbles with smoke inside. And the dripping plastic wand.
A frozen clot of noodles hanging from the brambles.

Equal? I suppose I shall. Which way?

Tapping a quail's nest like a tambourine.
A rustling in the air. Dawn over there.

Any way.

A bag of equal night, a scratchy burlap sack.
A paper towel rolling. A dark brown bean.

From *The Selected & New Stories of S.*
Story to a Clod [From *Stories to Stuff*]

Jealousy, now, but jealous of our younger, more handsome self.

Jealous of those perfect ones we've yet to meet. They're there, though.

Did we say ivy? Envy. January. A lampost with envy, our story

like a game of telephone keeps coming back unrecognizable

/what has happened to my story?/ an alphabet choking on air

on the scaly streetside, a hairy ring on every finger for every

day of the year—thin ring made from one hair tied to itself,

möbias, the falling of days like fish into tousled sand pockets,

the future failing, to be, to be the future, forgetting forever

about purpose, plan or place: the entire imbroglio of earthworms

Bus

I have swabbed the thick repellent under my eyes,
around my mouth—citronella & weak acid.
In my blazer pocket, a sachet of grounds: the limb
that crashed through the kitchen, the dust of a lost uncle,
delivered in a curious package, stamped priority.

We watched. They lied. They were nothing.
We waited, we watched & still nothing & then
you left so I watched & still nothing. They're late.
Was't to this end I louted & became

the menial of men, swayed by command,
a limb in a wind in a day? Washed my hair
in lye, until it began to burn, & long after,
until night came: passenger, blindfolded,
drugged, into the city—ready for anyone's
eventual return

•

season of the mite
season of the midge
splinter in the dancer's glittered midriff

season of a whiff—
nail-polish, season of the milk-bath

seasoned & scratched
in season, scratching raw, raw

season of claws
& clippings, of rose hips, of drippings on bread

season of a head
in a head & a drill on a bug & a sun in a cup

season to louse up
the quarantine house, season of minute hunting

season of wanting
the cache & the sash & the cinch; the underground bridge

season of the midge
husks sifted through cracked sand; of the mite &
of the midge

•

or so one story goes

The bus is free on Saturday
a lake where the drowned can go
gas bugs ahaze
at it   in it
The bus is free on Saturday

or so one story goes

unbreakable comb
collapsible womb
verdant seed of fatality
a man comes in combing
and behind him

•

I have draped the tight mesh about the portals.
It took a day to do & is not yet done.
Smacks of approval: early-evening stoking
the swarm of ash from early evening.
Early-evening bellows. Early-evening squeezing
its brass-hinged bellows.

Behind, always, evening, always evening
come to cancel brightest spore & medium,
come to raze in a sweep of sheer evening;
the rest of things: a thought caught in its matter

•

The secret to the vicinity shone clandestine. The wet flares. A slow news week,
smothered in furniture. The moon, or what we thought was the moon. I barely
       knew ye,
hostile environs, for I was furnaced. Flumoxed. Amidst the news which was the

news of my pores, news of a blunt instrument arose, I pushed seek
& found a voicéd wave. I spun the squelch dial, clockwise it took off the top.
The bottom remained, large as earth, as real, pregnable: cracks in blacktop,

abalone mineral caves sprung from a single leak. And the hollow cheek
of the hungry woman, the pits in her veins, the meager load, the dry canal.
The furrows her wheelchair carved in soft mud during a saturated fall.

It leveled with snow in winter, it fit a ditch in spring; now come to eke
a living from a skin & a scab, in a wave with the dry season . . . : the midge rises.
The collective midge, in formation, a massed mind, special prizes

•

The wheels	*the bus*
on the bus	*is free on*
go round	*Saturday*
& round round	*Saturday*
& round	*Saturday*
round & round	*the bus*
the wheels	*is free on*
on the bus	*Saturday*
go round	*Saturday*
& round	*on Sunday*
all around	*it don't*
the town	*run*

•

today I turned
today I turned divisible
a math as a prime moved into me
edifice my antennas scraping sky

I get the channels for free
some fluency a piece of it & it
flew into the blooming night
among the evening papers

some . . . into the blue blue night
'twas to be hours
our shoulder gapped the door
required some decoding

before it broke
before it broke it was a code
beautiful it was
early it was not riddled

it is
I am a mine
there are the yellow-orange bricks
of home shall I pull the stop-wire?

there is the street past
mine the one past that
the one past
the ones

but to the ones who truly require
to the ones who truly require this
honey, I'm home.

Manna

What first strikes us as so impressive is the utter lack.
It really is nothing & we have traveled so far to see it,
to put our tongues inside it, to smell its non-scent
& to preach nonsense to eachother, the already converted.

It really is something, though, the way you step into it
& become allthemore beautiful. It has a place in a popsong,
but the song is only one word long, repeated until the gaps
between the siren's skrees shorten. Until it is a steady howl,

& even the troubadour can no longer hear his word.
He cannot hear himself singing *refrain, refrain. . . .*

But it is somewhere in the mind.
At first it was a wise-ass statement on songstructure
but it became a plea: Refrain from your strange perfection,
it is placing the coin *us* recklessly on the railroad track.
I can feel it vibrating, soon we will be stretched long & paperthin—
Abraham Lincoln as painted by a third-grader with a good eye
for detail but lousy with perspective.

And now the only sound
is the slapping of a loose shingle on Mrs. Donaldson's rooftop.
She is ninety-eight & a political activist. Of course a widow.
A child of the child of the civil war. Yesterday she sent her first e-mail.
She is in love with me & what I could do with her lawn.
In here the laws of physics don't seem to apply: an egg
wobbles up the crooked counter; I flush a potato bug
pinched in tissue & the water whirls clockwise.
It wasn't supposed to be this way in America

but the only television program on right now is the mini-series
that seems to be about three owls trying to save the forest
from a rapidly rising black dough. Jeez, they look tired.
They spent yesterday pecking the pumpernickel
until it looked like a seabottom sponge. Then they took
it in their talons & dropped it in the drink. But tonight it's back
more amorphous & therefore more fearsome because it's night.
The owls become ingredients. In the swelling warmth
of the yeast ferment, their heads whir like dull drill-bits.
The trees & the drink & little hills become ingredients,
refrain, refrain. . . .

        This is a really good show.
Tomorrow, says the trailer, tune in
for the series finale in which all the ends are unloosened,
in which everything you thought your life was gets swallowed
into the bookends of someone's enormous sandwich.

City Ledger

So these are the publicity shots of our personal savior. And here is the residue's residue, & the list of twenty-seven miracles that happened to the eighth & least conspicuous ocean. Which is in this canister.

Here is the deed for the hill in which the gravel museum was built—in the excavation of which the eighth & least conspicuous ocean was found—twenty-four miracles still miraculously intact—on its surface the 8 x 10 glossies of our savior wobbled. We hung them on a branch in the sun & they dried stiff & marbled, so have some souvenir candy. Chocolate gravel, toasted rice.

When the museum collapsed & crushed third-grade day, the rogue architect was captured & strapped to a steel table. All four hundred networks were on it & shot their special bulletins into the firmament. The economy soared, never to return. The ocean-keeper slacked in her New Wealth & so misplaced our ocean. Four new restaurants opened with a variety of ethnic offerings, one of which featured a dish they would immolate & then set hissing on your placemat. Often the Iranian cook would race into the Calypso room & throw an egg in the air that wouldn't land. Stock in our city sold out in hours. Crime spread, but your idea of a crime may be different than mine. At bridge club Mrs. Waterson asked *can one live on a bridge?*

Third-grade classrooms dilated into computer labs or faculty lounges. In fact, the ocean was finally discovered high tide inside a blue water jug in one such lounge. The mothers against drunk driving designed signs & billboards that soon became ubiquitous: one was a red circle with a slash through it partially obscuring a pile of gravel. The other was similar, but said ARCHI/ /CTURE.

The evening I fed the architect's arm last sap he sighed savoring the savior role in its ultimate. The floor was smooth & cool. I was barefoot. How come. "Here we are," he said. Yes. A hundred cameras, fogging up the glass big time. I told Pete the apprentice to pull the foam socks off of the reporters' microphones, but only the colored ones. They were rows of flowers & reminded us of the earth, which we had once so admired for its ability to place a flushed lily right next to a fallen boulder of eagle shit. They're like dogs I tell you. Flying dogs.

Our Man

We knew we had our man when his limp switched.
And when the glove fit. And by his unusual hat size.
We knew we had our man when the ballistic tests
returned from headquarters. When the other glove fit.
We knew we had our man by the scratches around his eyes.
When the van of nuns gave their eyewitness testimony,
that's when we knew we had our man. We knew we
had our man by his guilty plea, & by his high-pitched
voice (which matched the tapes)—just like a woman's.
When we dialed up his web page. We knew we had our
man when we located the security footage, & voilà: our man.
Let the record show that we knew we had our man by the
blood dousing the scene, by the semen deposits, the prints.
We knew we had our man when we pried his trunk open
and found the grocery bags stuffed with horsehair beards,
bleach, dye, tan-in-a-bottle, the ransom note, the suicide
note, the travelers' checks, the unmarked bills, the bodies,
the bunk passport; the certificates of authenticity. Maps of steam
tunnels that span the city's subterrain. We knew when his alibi
didn't stack up—she had never seen him; his parents
(weeping their loss in their bests) never had known him a day.
When the other glove fit. We knew we had our man when
the contract shrink pronounced him saner than anyone
in the pine-polished courtroom, & when we showed
an epic of motive, but without a crime or victim
our man stumbled home sovereign, encumbered only by a row
of famished reporters, cars & buses feeling themselves
through the streets, corpuscular, a slight headwind.

Forensics

1

What was happening in the kitchen awfully.
How many chambers in the grinning gun.
When we surveyed the pink dot on the lanai's rail.
Where is the case with the conic sections in.
Why was it all congealing the autos spilled over.
Who really is Peter the Voyeur the getaway driver.
When it was happening were they aghast or what.
What is ball lightning anyway, hell's hail. Who are walking
nearer our inauspicious congregation. Why always this
the girders of the place look chewed
by moths in cloth & clumsy. Where the enormous intellect
that sputters out answers like a ground-meat grinder.
How is it going. When was the story named "Mysteries Explained"
                    starting:

   Lemme tell you somethin'! Do you know what you gotta go through if
   you're a witness? You gotta put on a shirt & a tie, drag myself downtown
   & hang around till the case comes up, which you never know when. And
      by the time it does, you forget what you was gonna say, & the other
      lawyer makes a monkey out of you! And it all goes on your record!

2

What we need is a crane & to chain chains
around this blood-soaked _____. The kitchen
workers hang from the vents with duct tape.
We need the _____ put on a slide, there were
signs of struggle. There is always some precedent:
You have heard, I think, about H.,
whoever he was, & how he met his death because his
father had too much suspicion . . . this you will not believe,
and I can hardly prove it, but I am that same H. . . .

You would not have known me, not in any part,
for I was simply one great wound. . . . Can you compare
your loss with my disaster—an enormous clear glass slide,
a landing pad for the _____. Cracked clear through,
splintered, blooddust clinging to tiny & numerous shards

3

Try to create an own legend
to gloss the map that extends
strangely understep. The grass
is browning swinging on the
roof of.   The ceiling.
The pavement hard & heading
between bent buildings.
An ice atom atoms are even
in the tugging air. Northwards
towards the axis pin. I am
a sling dusting for whorls.
Hundreds. Hair in a hanged man's
mouth a vernacular of fiber
a punctuation of blood, roots.
The map has no legend is only
a square of white fur. Outside
the square: the wall,
the wall, the cold wet red wall

4

Flowers. Dew hardens on & on &. How many first frosts
on us. Underfoot a rug of brittle plantbones.
At ten, I saw a man in a whitecoat pinch
a red rubber ball with steel tongs & dip it in a bowl
of steam. He hurled the ball wallward & it
shattered like glass. Was glass. Red glass, slowly melting
soft in the science center. We went to the aluminum
cone to watch the girls touch it. Eleven, their hair floats
like big wings up & everywhere. The electric surge

in the heart if I touched it—giggling, the girls are giggling.
Someone's intestine in a silver saucepan. Eager I look for
traceable blade ruts & fold it into a plastic bag.
Evidence hardens in or around us. Twelve,
a room an open wound, frothed with clues.

Peril, Perilousness

Since you were soso: a megadose
of the shrimp-pink pills Dr. ~
wrote the Rx for when this person
cracked 3 tarsals furiously kicking
townhall's brickwall, which
stood for something the second
before the e-wing at County
was shredded by a fearless power
or an unutterably powerful fear.

SWAT officers fetally folded,
blubbering gloopy their contact
lenses beneath the plexiglas lenses
that shield them from the hail
of parts: shingles, cinderblocks, cinders,
        bantam weathervane

hurled from the melting rooftop
of the prison burning. VFD vainly
hosing tons of water inside humancage.
Sheets of real smoke & teargas
fanned back sceneward by the sniper-
coptor's rotorblades. Dodging the
architecture, who will save the system?
And why why why?

(Not G, locked inside the prison library,
bladder bursting with scatology & treacle.

Not H, locked inside the prison library,
scrubbing the stinking stables, a penance.

Not I, in an air-cast to my calfmuscle, complete
with a phobia for even light.)

Inmates ignited to fingerlessness.
My foot throbs—tolerant to the liniment.

And somewhere you could be planting my pills
like mystery bulbs in the courtyard,

where the weathervane juts upside-down,
its inverted cock crowing good morning

—*what will spring bring & whence?*—

good morning, but good morning
on its empty blue-hot head.

From *The Selected & New Stories of S.*
[from *Miami Nights, A Fugue*]

Sometimes in Miami.
And sometimes not in Miami,
S. (not the author, not me) sd
Oh, my favorite book stinks
of decay, my favorite book is
now my least favorite of all,
of diapers, the enemy, its villages of mold,
sweating cover—Even the letters
that form its words, sometimes
S. says, have I found, finally,
to spell a host of unpleasantries.

Good, sd Chief, good, now we'll
throw the book at 'em.
. . .
Those Miami Nights.
how we spent them
and they us those balmy
Miami nights

although no one ever spun
campfire yarns about the golem
from the ground

although we lived
in a hut made of telephone poles
on the beach with no roof

our ankles matched
electric fence tattoos

Radio, Radio

In the middle of every field,
obscured from the side by grass
or cornhusks, is a clearing where
she works burying swans alive
into the black earth. She only
buries their bodies, their wings.
She packs the dirt tight around
their noodle necks & they shake
like long eyelashes in a hurricane.
She makes me feed them by hand
twice a day for one full year: grain,
bits of chopped fish. Then she
takes me to the tin toolshed.
Again she shows me the world
inside her silver transistor radio.
She hands me the scythe.

Re: Animation

Look at those trees, I said, *They are*
exactly as we would have them,
a flame jumps from one to the other
& leaves the last reborn virgin beech.
See the respectable rows they make
while their roots screw like spring snakes?

Now I am more knowing, knowing just this:
memory has made its moment.
I did it: replaced the original scenery
with a clay-nation landscape,
every color of the wheel swirled into the
plasti-scene sidewalks, homes & hills.
Changed the monologue, too: you are shameless,

Your nonstop stop-motion mouth breathing
that amphibrachic mantra; I am flattered
& embarrassed in front of all
these fixed witnesses—
you love who?—flicking a tear
as hard as a snail from your loamy eyelid.
We walk to the volcano like two hopping warblers

& dance like children to the singing of the local idiots.

Everything being identical, we are the idiots
& also their song. Camouflaged
against the sky, against the sound.

The solid sound laps the shore, somewhat silent.
We are that song: a sibilance, a sigh.

Do you recall the coda, the night
evaporating inward from the edge of itself,
leaving only me (always the last to leave)
to clean it up, to clean it up the way a mime does?

Tercets for Naiads

How I hope never to attend that party again.
Ah, but I will, will I ever always & inside Olivia
everything is happening in rapid succession.

Inside Olivia a little man pulls pulleys
& her mouth moves as if to speak so she
speaks her lines with an oblivion untempered

by temper or knowledge. She just met
the most amazing man & already he has
escaped her via the French doors & only remains

in the way that a close relative remains
months after the infamous disaster in Lake Placid
in the aftermath of the post-Olympic ice-fishing

soirée, which is to say she sees him cursing
fate silently through fogged plates & freezing.
My friend Jack jabs me & wonders if everywhere

is there such beauty, have we only noticed now
no longer encumbered by our consciences?
Fuck you, Jack, my conscience comes unclasped

everytime I wake up alone, & everytime I don't;
beauty is in the eye of the beholden, & the whites
of Olivia's eyes are as white as your oft-bloody nose.

But the models beneath that mural make
conflagrations of their drinks & drink them down
like rewound dragons! and the mural, the mural . . .

—means nothing but more wall, Jack, Sweet Half-
Glass-Full Jack, gone again for another refill,
leaving me with a mouthful of more words, which

I spit sub rosa into a bowl of disemboweled roses.
Olivia, that little man is your waterlogged father.
I see last words percolate & pop against the floe.

It's not the worst way to go, the cold numbs
the mind they say & whoever they are they
must have tried every conceivable way including

my own naughty fantasy: *Blanket of Bees,*
so outside for me where breathing gets easy
as air is involved with all of it. On powerlines

perch clichés so I curse them. I love them when
they prove me wrong again, bombing the bugs
burgling the lumens of the tenth traffic light

as if to say tonight eats today eats last night eats
yesterday. There is no traffic save each day Olivia
pacing kilometers closer & then miles farther away.

Some stars twitch in the swimming pool while
above on the board a stranger sobs. The music
from the mansion loses any sizzle & snap out here,

inside, acquaintances create chantey alma maters.
For the moment the moment is immortal & innocent.
Here comes Olivia with her wheelbarrow full of water.

Exoskeleton

Good the caterpillart is doppelgänging up on the tree
of north america as each character scurries toward
Interior Dramatics or are they watching their ochre guts
become their skin all around them armoring amouring

a romantic view of the future featuring an obscene
flight and pollination—all awls gouge the spitting ether.
The shitting weather. Out of the splitting heather
higgledy-piggledy heterosexuality of flowers miles

from more flowers. Sweet Sperm-shoes lands lightly
on a real wild tulip. Again & again we are not reminded
of sex but of the moments after when we are panting
covered with pollen thinking what is the next thing?

They might as well be in bags, the menswear's vinyl suits,
swushing as they spraypaint the cocoons with a thin
lacquer layer, crushing the creature as it swells with cells.

Wack-Ass Nesting Instinct

Perhaps not a syndrome but a drone of symbolism
(I've got myself surrounded) perhaps a sleazeball
Tethered to an Excaliburian goalie-stick, nonetheless,
I am pedaling my squeaky bicycle collecting scraps
That look like they would fit into my nest.

Perhaps not a palindrome but a month that unwinds
Like one, perhaps passing one's self on the bus speeding
Past one, nevertheless, nevertheless, I need to complete
My collection. This stick, frozen perfectly perpendicular
Into a mound of solid soil is one. Mother, you're too

Beautiful & clean to come for your annual visit.
Just you wait until you see what we've done to the place.
Bring some new mealworms, fresh socks, big boxes.
If I can pull this sucker out, cancel my conscience.

GoldStar for SONY Robotdog

Burnished one, hairless, animatronic one—one
chosen among the true ones, stalk-eyed, alloyed, dusted.
Ah, the pleasures of man—dawdling, dim, done & even
then the Company comes recasting roles & molds. Trusted
heads loll & Yesman's thumb allows, whorl pinning air.
Yes, & you Robotdog—impounded somehow sadder
than any spaniel, your blinking rods & pocked cones bare
before me—would not beg like flesh unless a matter
of my asking. Send a shrunken submarine to fix
my broken blood or like St. Bernard a bourbon thermos
necklace to keep me in my avalanche. You've a mixer
in your withers & a joy buzzer on your brisket to warn us
when we reach our limit. Of joy. A cocktail called a Molotov
simmers in your cistern. Fetch the remote, I'll switch you off.

From *The Selected & New Stories of S.*
excerpt from *Dr. Optimism, An Unfortunate Novel*

... then the gods of the gone meet the gods of the gods of the to-be-born, larval gods who've tunneled back through cakes of time to join the skirmish inside my darling's left ear to which I administer one bracken-green, Kracken-wet leech and gromp gromp the gods are eaten.

Some things do not exist anymore.
These are called "Dodos."

Some things do not exist.
The "Dittos."

Some things exist.
Herein our holiday.

Single Vision & Newton's Sleep

Lick the lights. Everyone
says that here. Sometimes
they'll call a spade a shovel,
hollowing half a hole,
which is all I have to sleep inside.

There's one

arboretum running
underground from near here
to Verisimilitude City.
I measure the macrocosm
with miles of mint string. Flossing

the dunning

skins from the incisors of the air.
The apples in our demi-dreams
drag themselves from the dirt
and into the indigo atmosphere.
Prime Mover, sleep. In the shade

ensnared.

Immortalities (dance remix)

Nothing was happening and
then it stopped. The charges &
temperatures were dropped. My hand
was an unfamiliar and
how it waved me hellos and
also how it caught & fanned

The cold drops off. In the sand
I thought of wines, flesh &
cash I had not had. I manned
space like a cosmonaut and
the fingernail of wasteland
I orbited had a grand

significance; notwithstand-
ing the rain it went. I planned
an ornate funeral and
I forgot. The mother &
daughter who made the cake &
favors called yesterday and

cactus quills pierced my lips &
ear. This pointed reprimand
did little good for my hand-
someness, little for the tanned
features I had fought for and
earned, here, my inaugural stand,

here, in this hurricane sand-
blast furnace with a burnt band
of tires bordering the land-
scape. You cannot understand

it, the darkness darning &
shredding the sky at once, and

If you can you must be strand-
ed here with me, nascent hand
in my ancient one, demand-
ing answers from a sky &
man that are very shy and
very far away. Please stand

there though: branded, moistened, and
plagued. It seems our life-spans and
the buzzards won't disband. &.

The Miscarriage

is absolutely another way to spend one's life.
So as I climbed out of my folded birdish body—
color & consistency of a stewed tomato—I
became my own precocious little brother & everyone

cooed, what a beautiful boy would have been & how
sterile it seemed under the saucerian fixtures, as in noonlight
our shadows gone or buried beneath us. Juiceless Fruit,
bouncing over drought-brown grass, crackling husk,

too parched to rot, momentarily mummified
then blown to dust; particulates of parts of dust—
some blew beside the curb & stayed there this morning.
Now there's nowhere left to live & people pace,

never see up or down but sometimes sideways off
the black window under the sign that says *Cremations.*
Minutes are coins no longer minted. Children fling
them onto the tin rooftops of their condominiums to seduce

their mothers with dreams of safe storms. The street is a strait
of funeral ships, dark impotent sails drag ever aft,
lacerating on the asphalt chop. I watch like an insect
becoming a stick. Like the eyes on the back of a green moth,

I watch half a moon boil in its tremendous kettle.
Something stripped every leaf, even the needles
from the conifers, & it wasn't winter. These bodies are not
our bodies but we pull them close to stall the shudder.

Duet

When I came to I came to.
The soap opera of tenor glycerin
bubbles snapping in both ears.

Then I came to a blue shower-curtain shawl
& in a foot of water.

My own starpainted body.
My own nonpointed stars.

I came to a sequence
of black-faced geese,
arching over me, surveying;
blotting out the lighthomes.

A skate grazed my hand like mucoused pumice.
My tic tacs on the curtain & on the water, cinnamon clouds
of fresh breath dissipating; spreading.

Pieces of pieces of Mercy Ship
fluttering, settling near me, defrosting my face,
disappearing.

At sea level, came to see the entire sea,
how it curved &
wrapped itself inside me.

a) Came to learn to grieve alone & not
   in front of anybody.

b)

c) Came to the light-black sky
   bobbing in its rusty canopy.

The Purgatorial

2 coal birds atop me
like an umlaut on a hieroglyph. Caw caw.
The subject comes: motion? A next what?
A? The signifying sky is clouding & looks us in, names us exactly:
2 birds.
      On a boy.
          Accompanied.

        On a mountain at the end of a sentence.
Note: knots of thin & uppity air: below the tree-line
the ante-purgatorial trees almost held things to eat.

Pausing at the lustful precipice. Why should we ever leave?

Remarkably it moved.
At the pay-toilet at the peak.
And a liquid-paper mist
suddenly exists,
a missing in the ink

("birds" are the nylon epaulets on my little yellow jacket.
Perhaps the man who will un-nest them both is already born).

I checked the snaps on my birds,
they are always flying away! Now
started everything in its place. An
infinitesimal sexual challenge,
small vanity momentous

as my still birth or first
step. As each cogwheel click

up this alp towards the 0
I need to be.

Heard it snows year round at this altitude &
                    yes it is.

Terrible flakes make
where they go.

I see through my leg & I stumble.

Below, the good people of Denver are everywhere,
making a dragnet, searching for the mayor's daughter.

But I am holding her hand. We made God wait.

We have been in love for thousands of years.
I go to kiss her but her mouth isn't

Fixed Horizon

I

inside the opposite side the same few things: meat-spackled ribs,
brown lung; the singular palpitating pouch. The symmetry of paint
inside a folded page—rending of cocoon, for purposes of flight.

•

Now you are approaching your initial destination, your initial destination.
Rest, born strange, climbing the ideal room: home in time for time at home.

•

That night the wind moved as if pulled. It filled every space,
it moved a hill over. It approximated music in a steer's skull,
& you tried to see it, where the eyes were. And then you saw it,
fixed horizon.

I I

Now someone knows what a line is. You try to teach them, the senses
are arced although. They trade laminated cards, pictures of the great composers.
The copper sun and copper clouds and rain's copper solder-strings—
kinds of weather. Still thirsty, they've committed the wine list to memory.
Your crimes were committed by another. They're still yours.
There's a tiny red tab in the crabgrass somewhere.

•

Any specialist will do. As a snake eating an egg finally has a head. The jaw
    detached.
As an egg being eaten has earned itself a body, spine as linchpin. Spine as
    periphery of spine,
as in: *on the periphery two stonemasons created a dirty joke. A spore blew from a
    fungus to a lunch brown bag—*

III

newspaper, *Daily Mirror,* which the governor reads from her lavatory / "satellite
     office"—
she has no stomach! "How can I concentrate with the tree doctors' saws?" she asks
her module, again, her spine sigmoidal despite the mediaeval childhood brace.
A lemniscus, a regular bundle of nerves. Inside, her cells spray her cells with mists.

•

A boy on his birthday has crushed his hand
in the knee-seam of a giant rat. Then sings & dances.

•

Fixed horizon, fixed horizon on the blackboard. This chalk is too . . .
too something: white, wide. There are cliffs of this stuff.
Comes to mind, through a diamond of chickenwire:
the garden with its annual harvest of snow.
Tall as it is wide (you wave your laser pointer—*Bless us*).

IV

Enough astronomy on the skin of a cup of tea. Enough time.
Everyone wants to be a marine biologist, drink a glass of water.
You're perfectly capable of throwing a chair in a room full of bouquets.
Crying until you get what you want. Reading a book about books,
a book about. You've climbed up the stairs, you've glided down,
quite rare thing. You've run your fingers along the seam of one of many earths,
felt a clump become another clump, felt nothing, but knew. The scenery blows
free, tangles in the scroll. A square of sod pulls loose like a tile.
The cables there, the tongues of trees licking. You were this close.
The planet moved.

V

Wings in it, enough astronomy to swim by swims by.
You're perfectly capable of navigating this blank channel,
of paddling past in the new, curved light, incessant dawn.

Stay still, stiller, still horizon, where you are—whistles
through your skull, an approximate music, near music,

not music,

•

waving the shore in

from the shore

From *The Selected & New Stories of S.*
New Stories

I

The new stories are like the old ones
only smaller.

I I

The new stories are like the old ones
only less ambitious.

I I I

The new stories are like the old ones
only more concise.

I V

The new stories are more representative
of the mind at work: a small, indolent, brief mind.

V

The new stories exist in zero gravity
or in an uncompromising wind.
A syntactical outline of the majority of new stories
would read: subject/verb/object.

V I

The subject of the new stories is always
themselves. The object is not the sublime.
It is sublime. The verb is *is* or *is* derived.

V I I

Unless the new stories trick their friends into
whitewashing the fence. Pranks of parsimony.
They float down the great river with African-American Jim.

VIII

Like a matte-green kitchen tile,
the new stories do not encourage
the use of simile. The new stories are
not metaphors, not exactly.

IX

The new stories searching desperately
for their mother in crackling field of hay.
New stories abandoned. For new stories.

X

The new stories set a record for field-goal-percentage
futility during the '87–'88 season.

XI

The new stories can be used to punish the ignorant
or reward the quick of mind. Or vice versa.

XII

The new stories: translatable as ground.
As gourds.

XIII

The new stories do it to you in your ear hole.

XIV

The new stories include a map to a trove.
New stories with thimbles on their vowels.

XV

The new stories are named after the sexy new ones.

XVI

The new stories wrapped around
two mysterious, long, cylindrical sandwiches.

XVII

The new stories as fading trinket:
a familiar, comforting scent
(the mint that parts the walk)
to the meticulous new reader.

XVIII

The new stories climb a silken rope
to freedom.

XIX

The new stories are not responsible
for the termites that feed on electricity
and fuck up your wiring.

XX

The new stories chirp & whistle like
a wet robot.

XXI

New stories treed at twilight.

XXII

Love Stories, Brain Stories,

XXIII

the new stories. The new. The.

The New Newness

The new newness: everytime or rather eachtime I open my
room to molt my accouterments—there: newer than newest:

I open my room: prosthetic jumble, petroleum limbskin shines.
Some plankton waves a UPC over a laser under a ceiling.

I open my room: cross-sect of green sea, silver weeds, baleen
approaching to strain me. Makes tiny meals but there are

much of us. Renew. Make it new. Repackage, reseal, revamp.
Renegotiate my contract. "Ben gone." Ben gone to *buy some brews*

It scanned well. They needn't re-enter. Need not need to. I'm over
21. A brand new brand. I braided my guts to brew. Make every

week shark week, but more missilelike, more serrated sharks. So hoppy
I bribed my guts with the new improved. I slipped on the credit slip.

I bruised my assbone. The new municipal park in the cityship
in the country is New Country Park: there is a blue cube for a powder

room: there is a hill where off season they are ranked in argent shelter
the new-yellow promotion stand is the WPIG *your rocking new country—*

strain me out. We do not understand it seems the bigger would be
the better meal. We don't have room. No room. Awakened by the

> the landlord's boot snaps a root
> Purple sun in the minnoweyes
> Falling down a waterfall!

Years of Age

Years of age pullulate like the elections again
& no idea where to register & one fool or another.
Like kids' games since the resplendent creation
Of injection-molded plastics. They send out shoots.
It's like you miss someone you've never met
So you buy some calligraphs & begin writing

Epistles to a specific no one but soon you're writing
To all of mankind, which you keep inside a shoebox against
The closet wall. Each page a year of age. Well met,
Mr. Doyle. Absolutely what the world needs: another
Sestina about time which uses its end-words to shoot
Itself in the randomly-running foot in re-creation

Of how our days get spent . . . & just what do you do for recreation?
I bet it's not this, but if you spend much time writing
Your congressman about your constitutional right to shoot
The neighbor cats that soil the sacred ground before your plastic Virgin again
& again, well, that's almost as bad. But that's another
Story. Isn't it almost empowering to spend these years of age with no Kismet—

OK, imagine you've met

One requirement for the creation

Of a perfectly good sestina, the end-words bite into the ass of the line one after another—

Gear-teeth—but when you finally stop & count the syllables of the lines you've been writing

They're jagged as the years were, the years of age. When we discuss poems, we say things like "too clever," & we mean them. The Reagan

Years were pretty enlightening ones for us, as the grainy, silent, super8 photoshoots

Suggest—the years we went from young to young men. But if someone shoots

A pistol at you, I don't know if I can take that bullet, I mean we've just barely met,

Dear reader, & I am most afraid of two things: death & growing old—come quick! They're at it again,

The kids from up the street, dragging their cheap neon snowboards to the top of the bluff, re-creating

A different season but it's summer so they grassboard & so fast & nothing can catch you. I'm writing

This from up here, second story, "the study"/living-room, but I want to be over there, I want another

Vantage point, I want to fall in that crazy dirt, to stain my play-clothes deep green & then I want another

Stain, this time my entire face, monstrous, dandelion smudge, buttercup, Indian paintbrush, mad shoots

Of *the hair of graves* shagging my head—perfect Propecia for the years of age, who are currently skywriting

Their cryptic names & dates in an different sky, not this one. We've also said "too strange," but comets

Come back like clockwork, the metals miles under our feet flow the consistency of milkshakes & creation

Is a myth. Over dollar drafts & bean burritos we discuss "the truth" & our multitudinous death-trips again:

In one of mine time is represented by luminous fractal meteors bouncing inside a pitch-black recreation

Room. I'm sizzling like a fajita on a chalk-bruised pool table. In another, multi-hued jellyfish legs shoot

Towards us, interminably, from a yellow & green sky. It's OK, really. I'm just glad you're writing again.

Weathers

It's freezing in the desert but there's nothing there to freeze.
The ground slides & swells. Where have you been buried?

Under which dune did you say? In the morning winter leaves.
Hush I can hear the aphids aphony & almost a word in the wind.

Time. Shovels. I'm late. I'm latent. I lost my list.
It was only "difference." Hailstone a lodestone on a leather lace.

Is there a certain lack of polarity? Is it family? Here I am.
In the cold moon's blast zone on clean sand & up is the deep murk.

Up licks my foreign shores. Tide of light. Hailstone beckoning
me to the brown ground. Something there, deep in the drift.

It's a piece of snow. Where have you been buried, oasis,
O trace H_2O? Hush already I can see evening leaving.

Atop this cactus the bees are hibernating. Hush they are dreaming
their communal dream, nothing. Sweet dreams. A storm took you here.

Your hive of snakeskins & spiny things. Sweet dreams bees.
Every morning winter ferments. Agent my eyes. May the bulb

of winter be planted deep enough not to burn may the blossom
return may the pollen swell & slide may the nectar mollify

•

There once was a hole in a stone.
Try as we might we could not see
to the other side. I put my

hand in the equator. It was
wet & quite warm. I placed my toe,
my leg, in the glazed equator.
My clothes listed from a brassy
hook in the wooden tie upright
in a stone. The air much cooler
now than the equator. My hips
slipped into the flat line of the
equator. You basking under
your tiara of succulents
on a stone, toying with a stone.
My red beard spread on the skin of
the equator. I drank of the
equator. The salt in that line.
I lowered my brain into the
planar equator. You began
to slide & swell above my sure
face, calcified, the equator.
I love you I hummed I can't swim

·

1) Take an orb, fallen into your habitat.
2) Slice an orb in two equal domes.
3) Take a leather line (a shoelace or such).
4) Place a line between two such equal domes.
5) Make an orb, product of your habitat.
6) Vice it by hand 'til it is compact & good.
7) Wake. The concussion of summer, searing the shadows.
8) Pace & watch for weather while the stone
9) slakes far beyond its molten core.
10) Chase the lodestar all (summer) day

·

Hush I think now I may
be the future:—

me well & working
at the technology hut,

you floating in a tall,
complimentary glass

beneath our domes
biogeodesic,

springing & falling
the same thing,

only difference, poolside—
our chair giving & low.

Vigil

Vigilantes murder Murderers.
Debutantes ball behind the bike rack.
The gang called Scissors wear lefty Fiskars
around their wide gold chains. The Rocks
wrecked them on Wednesday but they
were soundly smothered by the Papers
the following day. The Fires, come,
cauterize the few unlucky survivors.
Waters, flush them out, bury them at sea.
For a sign a wave that won't go away.
And on top of your gangs you've got your
gangs of Angels: Guardians in white berets,
Hell's pinching hogs between their jeaned legs.
Vigilant Vigilantes all, & screaming bloody
murderers. Doctors teamed to choke
a malignant growth, salt the salt, kill the killer.
And the namebadge, the tiepin with a goldplated
something on it, looks like maybe a syringe? —On.

Outside Busty Heart's Place even the Strippers
are stripping on their snowclothes [shift switch].
They ski towards me, & then in circles
around me, warm in ermine, barely there,
barely there. A snowball cracks on my parka,
a snowball with a thousand tadpoles packed
inside, out of season, a little frozen, a little soft.
A sprawl of punctuation on the unshoveled sidewalk

snow comma slush comma water comma period

The news nine trafficopter hides overhead like a tricky god,
crouched behind a cloud the color of a coors can.

Chopping up the bird formations, for instance the cedar
waxwings; the carbon-encrusted nightingale. The geese V late
going to Pensacola, Fla. The Personality plays with his wrist
splint & improvises inside my green AM headphones:

. . . well folks, from up here it looks like everyone

is going somewhere & you can read the city's age
like tree rings, although the east side harbors a large

vegetal tumor in its own east side. Arteries are clogged.
The canal's a string of dry silicone sealant,

you could use a bead on your windowframe . . .

The sun & its hair crumple behind me like a red drogue.
That's a little parachute. I've landed. I'm a good vigilante—
murdered some dots that won't become poison frogs.
I've landed. I'm a human being I'm a sex machine.
The bloodless heart of the bionic breeder.
A repetitive mechanical lunge.
Vigil: two-hundred-million-billion decisions a second.
Ante: endurance, equations, endgame, checkmate.
Frogspit dribbling down my insulation. Yolk. Birth plug.
Amniotic installations. Creative new packing materials
made from odorless molds. Broken water. Floating
deaf & helpless between two ridiculous saline tits.
God's posh silver sterile grave, in a cryogenic tube—
In Case of Emergency Break Glass.

And then I see a man running before a vine of ivy lights,
a child in his arms. I see rows of dull bells shift their weight
silently so far in the chapel's open-air attic

& I remember, hey

NOTES

"Forensics": the two longer italicized portion of the text are, respectively, from Archie Bunker and Ovid (Humphries trans.).

The italicized line in "The Purgatorial" is from Dante (Ciardi trans.).

Bottle in a Message in a Bottle; or, Afterwords

The blank, the tree debris sharded then shriven, the one
Sun so bright, no looky. The sun on ivy over
Glass, open the dermis; see all the people. Zoom in:
[900x]: the amoebae Church, air bubbles mass
At the entrance, elect ushered in by a flesh flap.

After having had words it's hard to say. Dark in here.
Our eyelids sore, & our lips—from the tattoo removals
& the new tattoos—bandaged. Remember? it was nice:
Hoi polloi sliding into the pressed suits & elocution
Of the haute monde, sounding out syllables & spaces.

And in each camp around an on coal an aurora halo
Of something noxious blooms. After words broke beside
The pool we threw them back, just to see. What is it?
Its name, possibly a picture, maybe some new thing? *

*/& the fish we ate that summer required no scaling/& the water we drank
has yet to be rain/